Journey on the Silk Road

Also by Lost Tower Publications

Poetry

Poems From the Witching Hour

Hope Springs A Turtle

Dog Days: A Celebration of Dogs

The Gift of a Rose

The Black Rose of Winter

Bridge of Fates

Purrfect Poetry

Eastern Voices

Journeys Along the Silk Road

Lost Tower Publications asserts its copyright over this book as an anthology.

However, Lost Tower Publications does not have copyright for the individual poems printed herein.

Each contributor has kindly agreed to have their work published by Lost Tower Publications within this anthology.

The copyright of any of the poems published within remains the copyright of the authors.

The copyright of any of the photographs published within remains the copyright of the photographers.

Lost Tower Publications are a small, independent publishers.

Our aim is to recognise and showcase exciting new talents in the world of poetry.

©2015 by Lost Tower Publications

For further information please visit:
http://losttowerpublications.jigsy.com

Journeys Along the Silk Road

Contents

Ava Bird	Haiku	13
Pamela Herron	...and I think of China	14-16
Carol J. Jennings	The Train from Guangzhou to Beijing	17
P.J.Reed	The Great Wall	18
Patricia Williams	Sketches Along the Yangtze	19
Martin A Willitts Jr	Rain is the Face of Desolation	20-21
Cigeng Zhang	Jungle Jewel	22
Pamela Herron	North of Kowloon	23–24
Elisavietta Ritchie	Searching Hong Kong for Chocolate, 1977	25
Neelam Saxena Chandra	Reverberations	26
Shouvik Hore	Rasulpur	27
Sonnet Mondal	My Chained Faith	28
Kristin Roahrig	Dance of the Drums	29
Aditya Shankar	A Tree, My Age	30
Sunil Sharma	Bonsai	31
Sunil Sharma	Mirage	32
Elisavietta Ritchie	A Surabaya Sequence	34-36
Ingrid Gjelsvik	Bonsai	38
P.J.Reed	Haiku - Japan	39
P.J.Reed	The Rising	40
Jasmine Kang	Kashmir Dream	41

Jasmine Kang	Still Water	42
Shittu Fowora	Kampung Blues	44
Elisavietta Ritchie	Chickens are Not Emotionally Satisfying Pets	45
Elisavietta Ritchie	Monsoon Lessons	46
Manuel Ortega Abis	The Philippine Cross-Stitch Society	47
Gonzalinho da Costa	Batanes	48
Gonzalinho da Costa	Afternoon has lost its fierceness...	49
Roseville Nidea	House Sparrows	50
Con Valenzuela	I Am Not Maria Clara	51
Con Valenzuela	Pick Up Her Hanky	52
Indunil Madhusankha Bassa Hewayalage	I am not Going to Prepare Kevun this Time	54
Indunil Madhusankha Bassa Hewayalage	Oasis	55
P.J.Reed	Haiku - Taiwan	56
Abhay K	Bangkok	57
Abhay K	Patong	58
Kai Coggin	Bangkok	59-60
Luna Swart	Salute	61
John Lambremont Sr.	Temple at Sunset	63-64
Kushal Poddar	Tour	65
John Lambremont Sr.	Triad Monitions	66

Journeys Along the Silk Road

Introduction

In its long history the Silk Road has seen empires rise and fall. The Silk Road has witnessed times of conflict and peace carrying a variety of exotic trade goods such as silks and spices from Asia into Europe and Africa and back again. The Silk Road brought new cultures, religions, languages with it, forever changing the countries it passed through.

The Silk Road is an ancient system of paths and camel caravan trails which have existed for thousands of years perhaps reaching as far back as Alexander the Great. In the first century Zhang Qian united much of the land through which the road travelled, making the Silk Road safer to travel and the flow of trade and new ideas rapidly expanded.

In the Han Dynasty, the Silk Road originated from Xian in China and went to Dunhuang where the road divided into three main routes. The Southern road spread through China to Kashmir and then into Pakistan and India. While the Central road wound around the 'Celestial' or Tian Shan Mountains, a UNESCO World Heritage site stretching through China, Kazakhstan, Kyrgyzstan and into Uzbekistan, The Northern road ran to the west along the northern foot of Tianshan Mountains, taking traders westwards towards Europe and the Mediterranean Sea.

Today the Silk Road runs through many different sovereign states: the economic sleeping tiger nations, war zones, peaceful democratic countries and military dictatorships.

The poems in the book reflect the exciting diversity of the cultures and people of the Silk Road. Drawn from countries traditionally associated with the ancient road, they offer a fascinating snapshot of life along the Silk Road in the twenty-first century.

The Great Wall of China

Ava Bird
Haiku

full summer
moon shadows
reflect Buddha
statues shapes

> rush hour
> inner city
> temple bell
> sings
> 'it's time'

full moon
brilliance
brings Zen student
to illumination
'don't be fooled
by ego'
said the teacher

...Thoughts of China

Pamela Herron
. . . and I think of China

Great Wall
Forbidden City
Terra Cotta Soldiers
Temple of Heaven
Middle Kingdom Tourists
gape, with cameras, from
air-conditioned buses,
thinking they've seen China.
Trapped in a dining hall
lazy susan with fries.

And they think they've seen China

Yangtze lazes brown and deep
cutting centuries through the
mountains. Ordered terraces
on the hillside, gathered lace of
orange trees, melons and
greens. Dinner still warm from
the sun. Basket hat masks the
face unchanging for centuries.

And I think of China

Security police, so very young,
crisp uniform, eyes forward,
Unblinking. See the foreigner
looking at you? To see if you
are looking at me? Red Guard
kerchief treasured at home
Did you ever giggle or play?
Will your children?

And I think of China

Hutongs hidden alleys sizzle
an evening meal. An old man
in cotton shorts fans himself,
sees me and stops. He nods
and fans again. Women with
baskets of fruit walk home
with no hand to fan.
Children laugh behind grey walls

And I think of China

China has always been, in ways
unknown To occidentals. Robert
Hooke in 1666 decreed the sun of
the western sky occido - Latin to
go down or set. The sun has set
on the Silk Road,
Artists, philosophers, inventors, writers,
5000 years before Mr. Hooke oriented
China in the East...
Winds change

And I think of China

                                      Historic
                                      Beijing,

                  Ancient
                  Xian,

                                        Modern
                                      Shanghai,

                            Bustling
                            Hong Kong,

Stone forests
Great deserts
Rivers run through

And I think of China

China cares what we
think, But they don't
have to. Do we care
what they think?
We will have to.
China closed doors for centuries,
because they could. Can we
open doors to the future,
because we should?
It won't always be ours to choose.

And I think of China

Golden years,
golden glow on
the bay, Mist
creeping over
Lantau,
Incense and
temple bells
America?
China?
America.
China. I long
for home,
a peaceful ending

and I think of China

Carol J. Jennings
The Train from Guangzhou to Beijing

From southern rice paddies
to northern coal dust,
for two nights and a day
on a crowded train,
we share a compartment
with a family –
the father going home to die
but unaware of his condition
states the Hong Kong doctor's
letter, written in English
that he cannot read,
but proudly shows us, the Americans.

His grown son and daughter
in People's Republic uniform blue
tuck their parents into lower berths,
spend the night on hard chairs
in the narrow corridor
(unable to pay for beds),
watch and listen as the old man's
body quakes with coughing
through the long nights.

The only Caucasians on the train,
my sister and I in our upper berths
play gin rummy and scrabble,
laugh like girls at camp.
For an hour in the afternoon,
we sit with the family
and watch farm workers,
who do not look up from the fields,
and children beside the track,
who wave us north,
and we all smile at each other
as we sip our flower tea,
having no common words.

P.J.Reed
The Great Wall

Walk with me she whispers
To a wandering breeze
Emptiness entices
As the great wall winds
Through the watchful trees
Ambered by autumns
Gentle caress and
Meanders through the
Sleeping, morning mist,
Following the path
Of a thousand souls
With a single step.

Patricia Williams
Sketches Along the Yangtze

I. Solitude
None save the glowing moon attends
ten thousand peaks along the river.
Lonely wanderers in the gorges
unabashedly weep for home
on hearing the echo of gibbons crying.
Only here can a traveller
catch sound this mournful.

II. Myth
The gorges are deep and long,
crowded with sheer pinnacles
so clouded that sunlight rarely penetrates,
green-clad and often shrouded
in a curtain of rain.

Here, an Immortal loved a mortal king
and invaded his dreams
as a cloud at dawn and rain at sunset.
Clouds and rain have since begotten
a symphony of longing.

III. Renewal
Ahead are the twelve peaks of Wu Gorge,
famed frothy, bleak, dark place.
The aura is heavy, sombre, desolate;
waves churn, roar and rush toward the sky.

Over the frontier pass,
wind and clouds sink to the waiting earth.
Traces of million-year ancestries
embrace ancient terrain;
the mighty Yangtze crashes,
carving its way to the sea.

Martin A Willitts Jr
Rain is the Face of Desolation

The inexpressive rain
lacks imagination, falling
wherever, without thinking
consciously of cause and effect.

The size of the rain is random.
It could last several days
and it would not matter,
the results would be the same.

What causes more concern
is the lack of rain.

When weather has no destination,
the day is unending.
When restless rain fizzles out,
it is not for the lack of trying.

The weather is trying many different aspects
of misery to see which one fits best.

Sometimes, it is the surface of silence,
small as a pinch of salt.
Sometimes, it is knocking on a door
no one answers.

Sometimes crows discuss the weather
as a source of blackness.

It is fall. Rain is practicing chill —
like monks not sweeping a courtyard
wishing not to disturb anything.
Rain pings against my window
with white shavings of crane feathers
unrelated to stone.

Those monks are not monks,
but cranes attaching torn paper napkins
into clouds.

Footprints of rain on a long journey,
hesitate. This is why
rain lingers like a rejected lover.

Hopelessness—
rain saturating the bottom of a canoe
while I do nothing.

Monsoons wrinkle on my face.
It is already too late.
The nothingness is here,
drenching everything in sight
until it is hard to see far.

The sky empties its belly.

Only the water spider can walk in this,
and then only with extreme care.
For what is transparent
hides what is underneath.

If I was any more miserable
I would have company.

Cigeng Zhang
Jungle Jewel

Lush trees
Towering into the clouds
Leafy in green
A ceiling of spring

A red bird
Fell on the branches
Singing a sweet song
Like a happy bride

Shining leaves
Danced like butterflies
Soft breeze
Whispered in tropical rhymes

Beautiful orchids
Brought amorous feelings
To pick some wearing on the neck
A floral necklace-- oh look

Pamela Herron
North of Kowloon

slide open the door
of the berth in car 14
to see the warm welcome
of snowy, crisp ironed
embroidered sheets

spotless bedding that
doesn't know or care
whether we are domestic or
foreign visitors riding a train
thousands of miles from home

I rest my head
against the cool window
as fragrant jasmine tea
steams my face
and the view outside

as the sun dips
below the horizon
the train is rocking
back and forth lulling
my family to dreams

in the distance
three railway workers
squat by the tracks
a brief respite until
the train passes

one tired man on the end
takes off his straw hat
face lined and worn
his idle gaze lifts up to
the cars of the passing train

our eyes meet
I smile and lift my hand
in silent greeting
his dusty brown face
breaks into a return smile

as the train jolts past
his eyes widen in surprise
the last thing I see
he startles from his reverie and
slaps his companions' shoulders

waving his hat he points
a frantic gesture at my car rapidly receding
his two companions raise their eyes and
look up at passing cars in curious interest
not seeing me at the window

his eyes follow the train as his hat
drops forgotten at his side
I see him tell of saying hello
to my pale face in the window as our train
grows smaller and smaller in the distance.

I watch too my hand against the cool glass
until there is no more trace of the three workers
standing by the track watching
my fingertips still rest reflected now
on the window as my family awakes

the tea is still hot
as I fill their ears with the story
of our brief meeting, the story
my friend will tell
over rice tonight.

...Thoughts of Hong Kong

Elisavietta Ritchie
Searching Hong Kong for Chocolate, 1977

The Chinese word for chocolate
is indecipherable.

Booked alone in a tall hotel,
1977, caught in the interim

between two husbands, two lands,
two lovers distant and dying,

I must find chocolate,
or else a doppelganger-

To find poets my business here-
but everyone here in shipping and trade.

Any chocolate imported must
have melted away in the heat.

Few speak my language,
None know my name.

To discover chocolate, lover or poet,
would be like sighting a pistachio sundae

while lost in Mongolian desert wastes.
I hunt through streets pungent, molasses-thick...

My tongue bound in splints and rags,
loneliness wraps me in my blue sarong.

Neelam Saxena Chandra
Reverberations

A voice reverberates-
In the heart imprisoned
Imploring to be set free;
Begging with folded hands
To be paid heed to.

A voice reverberates-
The implores slowly transform
Into squeaks and shrieks
Trying hard to break the shell
Into a land of liberty.

A voice reverberates-
Do hearken to the sounds,
The hapless voices
Before they melt
And pour out as lava.

All voices of revolt
Do not begin as a renaissance
Some begin as feeble voices
Which erupt as tiny bubbles
And become gigantic someday...

...Thoughts from India

Shouvik Hore
Rasulpur

Here are the banana leaves of my village;
Beneath which playing our childhood passed,
Sometimes at a distance one chastised sage
Would profoundly for hours there meditate,
Thankfully, such seclusion wasn't our fate!
With companion sisters in fields mild- grassed,
In games fully lost- though sights of a snake,
Climbing its trunks spread panicked excitement,
Then tired jumping in our ancient lake,
Arose late; when finally homewards plod,
Often watched a drowsy pilgrim under her shade,
Still were her leaves with humility bent.

When memories start to dissipate, fade,
I realise in past pleasures the presence of God.

Sonnet Mondal
My Chained Faith

The far-flung whistle of the colliery
and of the Calcutta-mail
calls me every day after dinner.

The train's shrill echo and
rhythmic melody of wheels
form a sublime image of
the girl out of my dreams,
waving and smiling;
screaming and crying;
standing and waiting
just for me amidst grasses,
trees and hedges that wave
in solitude and hope.

The curvature of the lopsided land
plays hide and seek along with
the clouds and moon blurring realism.

My belief is incurable and so is
the facade of pleasure that I show
while I follow compellingly,
the whistle of the colliery.

My faith lies in the train,
in the wilderness and
the vaporous figure of my love
while my whims are chained
with famine and society
that may identify me as a mad
once I leave my job and run
into the hazy backwoods.

Kristin Roahrig
Dance of the Drums

Round and round,
twirling to the sound
of the drum that beats the dancer's tune

The whip in the dancer's hands
beats against the drum
as yellows, greens, and reds
spread all across this Buddhist festival

Fabrics move amongst the other,
weaving in designs not bound to any form
they flow above the painted masks
of entities rarely seen
except at festivals such as these

Round and round with open smiles,
cloth tongues sway between the performer's teeth
Delighting in the dance of the drums

Aditya Shankar
A Tree, My Age

I wait in a queue and learn to age like the trees. It is a surprise that we stay behind each other, but no more turn into a toy train that sped through the fields and took us to the trees. Our stillness like the boats in the dock, not roots – restless. A stillness of its own kind, like the pounding heart beneath the blubber of the dead seal. A heart that forgets to express its subtleties.

While I walk through Bangalore, a tree my age gives me fruits and flowers. And all I do is keep collecting tickets at the end of the queue, scribbling poems on its rear.

Sunil Sharma
Bonsai

A small banyan
Sprouting in a pot,
A miniature marvel,
A little Japan being cultivated daily
In our Indian middle-class homes,
Two cultures collide in the enclosed spaces,
Creating a novel synthesis, fresh Asian voice,
For the global citizen, on the move,
Savouring new artefacts in
His rich drawing-room.

Sunil Sharma
Mirage

A construction worker
In evening clothes,
Thin tall body encased
In blue jeans and a red T-shirt,
Old footwear,
A different version
Of day clothes, stained and patched;
Talking on cell-phone
To somebody beloved,
Under the deepening shadows
Of the concrete-glass skyscraper
In the Mumbai suburb,
The cell phone,
Only gesture to affluence.

Stone Guardian at Sewu Temple, Indonesia

Elisavietta Ritchie
A Surabaya Sequence

Beyond Surabaya

Mountains hover like clouds
above clouds and town.
Were they uprooted eons ago?
Typhoons could blow them away.

The stream through the ditch
where silky brown families bathe
is more permanent
than those old volcanoes hung high.

Rootless in blue, we also enjoy
illusion, yet we know
the persistence of footloose peaks
beyond clouds of time...

Night Life, Surabaya

Mangoes hang green in the moon.
A cockroach bisects
circles of stone,
slices of moon.
Bats cast parabolas
over mosquitoes.
Giant plants meander on stilts,
shadows agitate walls.
Grass trembles with ants.
You sit tranquil as mangoes
ripening high in the night
until a flute splits our skin.
You take my pencil
and begin to write.

Krishna's Painting

Two purple suns whirl
in a greengold box
imprisoned for siphoning

night from the sky
through radiating flagellates,
then turned the world brick.

Old suns, yet
they still inject
your purple blood in me.

Beneath the horizon, earth
runs in underground rivers of ink.
The sky is ripe avocado.

Wednesday Night Surabaya

Geckos scuttle overhead
across red tiles.
I feel the body's tyranny.
Past midnight
through the open door
a large dark cat pads in,
curls in my sheets.
He dares me to displace him.
He wears your eyes
and we remain in my thin bed.
Geckos scatter red tiles overhead.

At Jago Temple

Be silence, you write.
I become gray temple stones.
You tear away lichen and moss.
Your fingers decipher

my hidden inscriptions.

Away from the sun, I keep
my colour of dried blood.
On broken heights I am
your gate to climb the sky.

Above Jago

The bird bears the turtle away on his back
high above waiting foxes and dogs,
the threat and warmth of earth.

He commands her silence:
one word –
she will plunge toward the tearing teeth.

She hooks tiny claws in his feathers,
hides her beak in the down of his neck,
rides for miles through the toothless sky.

Siwya Guru, Singosari

Only Siwya the Teacher remains
in his niche in Singosari.
The other gods have departed.

Siwya's hands broke off at the wrists
but his face beams through the gloom:
he knows his power endures.

Yet he teaches us only a shard
of his wisdom. The rest
we must find for ourselves.

Perhaps too late: Siva the Goddess
lost her head nearby in Jago.
And so have we.

Hamarikyu Garden, Japan

Ingrid Gjelsvik
Bonsai

tiny
transparent bowls
flowery food

friendliness is
a colour

silence
a tone

arigato
a word

silky sounds of
quick footsteps

...Thoughts of Japan

P.J.Reed
Haiku - Japan

Fragrant cherry blossom falls.
Pink clouds of perfume
- Startled sparrow sings and flies

    Falling raindrops draw circles
    On ponds still water
    -Green tree frog sits and croaks

Yellow sunflower paintings
Scattered on green fields
-Okayama industries.

P.J.Reed
The Rising

Warm red glow,
Slowly, spills over
Sleeping clouds.
Floating softly,
Falling Leaves,
Dance to the floor.

Pale ice spiders
Weave frozen webs.
Tall trees sleep
As green fingers
Of buried life,
Push through
A melting soil.

Darkness spreads,
In Shades of blue,
Softly wrap the sky
As forest sentinels
Keep look out
For the
Red glow Rising.

Jasmine Kang
Kashmir Dream

Heaven into earth, from afar
Rose a peak lit with hues of blue.
Within blue tints of cloud
Was an angel that sprang from a dream
Who sat on puffs of white cloud.

Streams of shooting stars sprang
Across the Heavens
As I closed my eyes and thought of Kashmir,
Whose face I did not know,
But had captured in a dream.

As if I were swimming
Through the starry night,
I saw myself with wings.
She was an angel.
All along I knew
There was something about her.
I saw it in her redemptive beauty.

This is the breath and light of Kashmir.
She guides her people
Through every struggle and tragedy
With hope and faith.
She knows that one day
There will be peace.

...Thoughts of Kashmir

Jasmine Kang
Still Water

Ever sweet is thy smile
That clings onto me to embrace
These forms while sweeping away
To the high mountains.

Light is in this lone cypress,
Whose branches touch the pebbles
Of the land and wildflowers
As the snow falls in winter,
As the water of Dal Lake turns to ice.

Eternity,
The stillness
Of a moment,
And still there is
Movement.

For a few moments,
Time shall stand still
With these colliding snow storms
And the turbulence of the rain that falls.

With a trunk bleached white by winds,
The soul of the cypress holds on
And stands like still water.
Just so Kashmir remains strong
With her song for peace.
It will not die, it will be heard.

Petronas Twin Towers, Malaysia

Shittu Fowora
Kampung Blues

I am talking to you
You are not hearing

I am begging you
You are not agreeing

I am pricing
You are not accepting

I am thanking
You are not minding

I am loving you
You are not responding

What I will do now,
For you to hear, agree, accept and respond to my proposal?

...Thoughts from Malaysia

Elisavietta Ritchie
Chickens are Not Emotionally Satisfying Pets

As I learned in a lone Malay hamlet,
final year of a marriage, fowl are not
loving, like cats, which he banned,

nor companionable, like the mutt
he got third-hand after I chased out
a midnight burglar while he slept.

Burnished auburn, emerald and gold,
the rooster strutted with audacity,
wattles wagged contempt for humankind.

The black hen might have felt
primordial compassion, for
day after day, no matter that

the door was to stay shut,
in she'd slip, rooster in pursuit,
stalk upstairs, leave her gift:

one beige egg, laid on my pillow
or in my bureau drawer
left open by mistake.

Were these fertilized?
Could I have incubated them,
turned foster mother to a flock?

But I recalled an adage,
Don't try to teach
your grandma to suck eggs,

found my darning needle, poked
a hole in the narrow end,
gulped the rich and slimy life inside.

Elisavietta Ritchie
Monsoon Lessons

After silence of drought, such speech.
From ephemeral alphabets traced in the mud
I'm learning the grammar of rain.
linguistics of flood.

But puddles are illegible
or too murky for strangers to read:
some message about pain
in the wet stammer of weed.

The sun declares the lesson over.
Hardly mastered. In dried ground
spelling crumbles. There remain
only punctuating buds around

what had been sentences. Next storm
I may learn to decipher earth's half
of cloud's thought, or fail again
to finish one fertile paragraph.

Manuel Ortega Abis
The Philippine Cross-Stitch Society

Everybody wants to marry a lover,
not a friend: because everybody knows it is forever
again and again. Everybody wants to relate to a movie,
not watch it: because everybody knows the
story and its pitch. Everybody wants to stitch a cross
in time, because one does what one does in rhythm
and in rhyme. Everybody wants a Philippine society
of weavers, not warriors: because there is business
in patterns and unity in
colours.

...Thoughts from the Philippines

Gonzalinho da Costa
Batanes

I am a traveller
In my heart
To a place of sky and sea-
A sky so pure,
Deepest blue,
Sea, same colour
As the sky-

Not so distant
As the farthest reaches
Of the earth or so
Inaccessible, yet
Sufficiently remote
So that solitude
Is a lone bird
Hovering

And silence
Is the expanse
Between two grey islands
Barely visible
As you stand
Atop a cliff
Dropping steeply
Down to shore.

Breakers whisper
As I breathe in sweet air.
Inhaling to my fill,
I lose all appetite
And dine on the wind.
No longer corporeal,
I am a subsistent soul.

Gonzalinho da Costa
Afternoon has lost its fierceness...

Afternoon has lost its fierceness like the death of summer grass, dry and crackling underfoot.
Dappled shadows fuse, separate, and coalesce- grayly shifting furtive forest animal.
Faintly the wind rises, gently kicking into circular motion fronds spinning in the liquid eyes of ponds.
Branches wave back and forth, swings, doors opening and closing, leaves entering and leaving.
Black asphalt roads glow, windswept dark coal fed by hot billows firing an old bronze censer.
Orange cats, writhing, lithe, play on jade grass, shiny crabs jostling, toys scattered at day's end.
Trees, outspreading dream catcher nets, poise against the horizon, tracing graceful fractals against the sky.
Daylight reddens, crushing pink roses against white cheeks of clouds.
Weakening, the hour bathes in vermilion blooms drifting in the darkening ocean.
Threatening black outbursts, thick clouds close to shore migrate toward the sun now deepening crimson with fatigue.
Remotely, obscured by a diaphanous curtain of rain, boats fade in and out, motes on a planetary visage.
Pummeled by distant turbulence, outlying storms, swirling fists, hurl violently into a far constellation.

Roseville Nidea
House Sparrows

The sun was about to set,
The house sparrows were all over
The lean branches of the evergreen mango tree;
At the balcony near the wild garden
I sat, on the corner of the old wooden chair,
In silence, I listened to their voices-- so sweet
So soft, so melodious
Nothing was more blissful than to hear
Them, singing in unison,
A family of small brown-grey birds was gathering,
Was sharing the comfort of their small home
Before the night would take the light,
They would all be shaded by the twigs,
By the snug of the leaves of the unselfish tree.

Enchanted by the euphonious twits, I stretched,
Both my legs reached, pressed hardly the rough
ground;
The loud whistle of the kettle suddenly
Called my attention to return to the place
Where I prepare, where I cook the food,
To pour the boiled water into the slim, sky-blue thermo
jar,
That was for the black-brew of the king after dinner
And I must do it at once for after few strikes
Of the hand of the old grey clock
Hanging on the painted wall of the family room
He and my prince would again be home,
Sure would seek the comfort of my warm hands.

So, I went back inside the house
Before the night took the day.

Con Valenzuela
I Am Not Maria Clara

outpour of femininity
anticipated by most women
refinement and politeness were the rules
this was my training
show sophistication in all ways
I couldn't move!
I couldn't breathe!
It was a fatal time in my past
the book said:
"put Maria Clara on a pedestal"
she deserves the honour of men
but I am not her
the picture of a true Filipina
demure and self-effacing
nuns pushed me
priests honed me
I was fearful of their wrath
I followed Maria's ways
I've kept my aggression and assertion
I was trapped in her imagery and grace
but my soul was my own
screaming wildly
dying to be me
dreaming to be wild and free
her downcast eyes showed she was shy
I am a parody of her coyness
but I have chosen who I am

I am NOT Maria Clara

I am

ME

Con Valenzuela
Pick Up Her Hanky

a Filipino tradition in courtship
the lady drops her hanky
the man will pick it up
he should take the hint
that it was done with full volition
their eyes met
they start with a smile
then a brief sweet talk
her eyelashes kept batting
as if there's a great romantic wave in her eyes
she saw her Adonis
she giggled discreetly
hiding her sensual eyes with her wooden fan
they wait for time to pass
the months turned to years
falling in love but in slow motion
when can he touch the hand of Maria Clara?
what about a warm embrace?
a kiss will be the highlight of their true love
wait! Pick up the hanky first

Giant Buddha, Gal Vihara, Polonnaruwa, Sri Lanka

Indunil Madhusankha Bassa Hewayalage
I am not Going to Prepare Kevun this Time

Loku Naenda sitting still on a bench
watched the framed photograph
of her son, my cousin,
that made an exhibition of him
in his army uniform and fortitude
My puerile questionnaire had its flow
as usual
One question of mine
received an answer,
which obviously touched my heart

"Wouldn't you prepare some *kevun* for the new year?
The nicest, your *konde kevun*."
"No *putha*, I am not going to prepare *kevun* this time,
What *kevun* for me?
I have already lost appetite."

As her speech came to an end
she returned to the photograph
and traced the contours of his figure
with her quivering fingers.

This time the *koha* didn't sing
its ritual new year song
in its seminal tone
Only the strident,
reedy tune of the crows
hobbling in the compound

...Thoughts from Sri Lanka

Indunil Madhusankha Bassa Hewayalage
Oasis

All the living are a caravan
caught in the sterile desert of suffering
Embattled in the timeless
sansaric journey
Sans a purpose,
quite unaware of a way of crossing the desert

The Buddha, the most fabulous of all teachers
Now is in the oasis,
having circumvented the barrenness

Renunciation,
as the Blessed One preaches,
clears the path to the salvation,
to the Oasis,
located beyond the arid desert of suffering

Glossary:
Loku Naenda - The eldest sister of one's father
Konde kevun - Oil cake
Koha - The cuckoo bird. It announces the arrival of the New Year from the beginning of April.

P.J.Reed
Haiku- Taiwan

The little cloud spills-
Bamboo sways and softly chimes
While warm raindrops fall.

Orange sunset paints
Over blue sleeping waters.
-Sun Moon Lake, Nantou.

The earth is waking-
Pathway crumbling underfoot
As ground shakes and groans.

...Thoughts of Taiwan

Abhay K
Bangkok

Dystopia

A maze
of stone, cement and steel
of highways
and high rise condominiums
equipped with miniature pagodas
housing guardian ghosts and spirits to guard.
My streets littered with massage parlours
and shopping malls.
My angels ever waiting
to amuse flesh hungry guest-gods.

Utopia

A distant Ayodhya
where king Ram still reigns
Indralok-- a heavenly abode
where Indra still rides
Airavat- the cosmic white elephant
An earthly Sukhawati
--the paradise of joy.

...Thoughts of Thailand

Abhay K
Patong

A promenade of rainbows
ensconced by emerald hills
sand silver white
fine as flour
sirens emerging from the Andaman Sea
as Botticelli's Venus.
A marine garden of Eden
reflecting azure blue sky
blobs of clouds
occasionally embracing the sparkling sun
sea waves calm
mild winds
myriad tongues
wagging on the babel beach.

Kai Coggin
Bangkok

Nothing of Bangkok
resounds in my bones,
no smells,
no sounds,
no images etched onto the rice paper of my memory,
the passing light
of Gleaming Golden Imperial Dragon Barges
gliding down the murky central khlong,
the dirty river marketplace of softened produce
sold from leathered old women in congested tiny boats.
The Golden Barges of the King making waves,
rocking the floating fruit huts, souring in the heat.

Nothing of this is from my memory,
I am putting together pieces as I write,
and creating a scene in my mind
that is dressed like a memory,
but Bangkok may as well be Alaska
cold in its un-remembrance,
like I was never even there,
like I was not born at
โรงพยาบาลจุฬาลงกรณ์
(King Chulalongkorn Memorial Hospital)
on the first day of the year,
on the first year of the decade,
the first child in a marriage that held desperately to lasting.

Trauma does funny things to memory.
Inserts clouded grey areas,
Sometimes over whole years.
Loses connections to colours,
but I know from pictures that I wore a
different coloured gingham print dress to school every day,

Monday was green, or Tuesday blue,
I know for sure Friday was yellow,
I always loved the yellow one because
the yellow and white blended into sunshine and didn't look so gingham,
and Friday was yellow, or Thursday,
and my face looks so happy,
I can almost smell the rust on those monkey bars,
but don't remember that I could climb them.

When Bangkok was ripped
out of my seven-year-old hands
and my father went away with my country,
I dropped all my memories out of a tiny hatch
in the airplane headed for America,
just let them slip from my tiny fingers,
underneath my over-sized seat,
each one falling through the life preserver,
through the cold cloud-covered metal of the airplane belly
and into the oblivion of sky and the widest ocean I have ever seen,
but don't remember seeing.

Luna Swart
Salute

I closed my eyes and the
5am Bangkok sun
Kissed my forehead
Through the tinted glass
Of the window on the 13th floor

Welcome
It said

Held hands up
Breathed in the light
Bowed to the sun

Finally
I said

Street market seller, Vietnam

John Lambremont Sr.
Temple at Sunset

Lady Buddha rises,
alabaster gleaming
over koi lake reflections,
embers of a dying sun.

Higher than an elm,
her face in silhouette,
smiling in mystery.

Chants from the temple,
our ceremony done,
another underway.

Vegetarian repast
passed among us,
satisfying, but all still missing
Grandma and Grandpa.

I am the foreigner here,
once shunned, later to become
Uncle John (you know,
the American one).

A monk clangs a bell
to signal the sun is gone;
Lady nearly dark now,
but ever presiding
over these holy grounds.

I slip away,
peruse her majesty;
over a cigarette,
to myself I say:

"Mom" and "Dad,"

I took your daughter away,
but that choice was yours.

Thanks for learning to forgive,
for treating your daughter's lover
like a son or a brother

In return of your kindness to me
I gave you beloved grandchildren, three.

...Thoughts of Vietnam

Kushal Poddar
Tour

A slow fast food cart, hand-rolled
Down the Ho-Chi-Minh city,
Arrives with some rice flour flowers
Afloat in yellow sweet syrup.
A little humid buzz rings.
Two bicycles to and fro,
Grey herons, coloured pigeons.
My fingers, my fingers, all
Has this sugary stickiness.
Figures merge, shadows part, I
Ride a serpent, stroll down
An alley. A needle-man
Promises to alleviate
All pain. The panes open close by.

John Lambremont Sr.
Triad Monitions

Take care in the disposition
of your broken-off hair:
if a bird finds one,
and weaves it into its nest,
the rest will fall out.

A turtle in your yard
is the best form of luck;
to tease or hurt it risks
a horrific twist of fate.
Give it good passage,
and see it safely
on its way.

Give thanks, and ask forgiveness
of all you must kill,
whether a stalk or leaf to be sliced,
a fish you may take from the lake,
a red hen whose neck must be wrung,
or whatever it is you need to butcher;
for there is a reason why
a condemned frog crosses
his supplicant front legs
in the last moments before
the cleaver falls.

Acknowledgements

Pamela Herron: '. . . and I think of China' was first published in *En l'air,* (Unsolicited Press, 2013) and is reprinted by permission of the poet. P.J. Reed 'The Rising' was first published in *Hope Springs A Turtle* (Lost Tower Publications 2013). Martin Willitts, Jr.: 'Rain is the Face of Desolation' first appeared in *Moon Magazine*, reprinted by permission of the poet. Elisavietta Ritchie: 'A Surabaya Sequence' was first printed in the *Ann Arbor Review*. Malay and Indonesian translations of 'A Surabaya Sequence' were published in *Berita Buana* 1997 and *Budaya Jaya* 1978; the poem was reprinted in *Raking The Snow* published by (Washington Writers Publishing House) © 1982 Elisavietta Ritchie. Elisavietta Ritchie: 'Chickens are Not Emotionally Satisfying Pets' was first published [Oberon 2002] Reprinted in *The Spirit of the Walrus*, (Bright Hill Press, 2005); *Awaiting Permission to Land* (Winner of the Anamnesis Award), *Cherry Grove Collections*, (WordTech Communications, Elisavietta Ritchie © 2006); *Feathers, Or, Love on the Wing*, (Shelden Studios, Elisavietta Ritchie © 2012 Shelden Studios) Elisavietta Ritchie: 'Monsoon Lessons' was first published in *The Christian Science Monitor (*circa 1977 or 1988); It was reprinted in *Raking The Snow*, (Washington Writers Publishing House, ©1982 Elisavietta Ritchie); and the *Fresh Water* anthology, (Puddinghouse Press, 2000)

Biography of Poets

Manuel Ortega Abis was the Writing Fellow at the University of the Philippines in 1992. He is now a Fellow at LIRA (Linangan sa Imahen, Retorika, at Anyo), in the Philippines.

Ava Bird is an American based poet, writer, editor, reviewer, producer, magical elixir maker and more! Her poetic works are printed in historical anthologies, academic journals, spiritual and online publications. She has published two collections of poetry and prose *The New Now* and *Rage Against the War Machine* and is an organizer for the worldwide poetry movement 100thousand poets for change. For more information visit her at https://www.facebook.com/avabirdpoetic

Neelam Saxena Chandra is an Indian bureaucrat working with Indian Railways. She has published nineteen books, including two novels, one novella, four short story collections, four children's books and eight poetry books.

Kai Coggin is a poet and author of *Periscope Heart*, born in Bangkok, Thailand, raised in Houston TX and now living on the side of a mountain in Hot Springs National Park, Arkansas.

Gonzalinho da Costa is the pen name of Joseph I. B. Gonzales, Ph.D, lecturer at the Ateneo Graduate School of Business, Makati City, Philippines and is the Managing Director of Technikos Consulting, Inc. He writes poetry as a hobby.

Storyteller, poet, freelance writer and editor, **Shittu Fowora**, is a lifelong fan of history and the power of scented words. He has recently been motivated by the winsomeness of birds and the wisdom of ants. Having been stung more than twice while attempting to lounge in trees to write verses, he now spends more time around PCs and electronic gadgets. He enjoys sharing ideas, verses and stories with those who care.

Ingrid Gjelsvik writes her poems in Norwegian and translates some of them to English.

Pamela Herron is a writer and educator in El Paso, Texas who frequently travels to China for research and pleasure. Her work previously appeared in Lost Tower's *Dog Days* anthology. Her collection of nature poems, *En l'air*, was published in 2013.

Indunil Madhusankha Bassa Hewayalage is currently an undergraduate in the faculty of Science of the University of Colombo, Sri Lanka. While his major engagement is with the disciplines of Mathematics and Statistics, he is also passionately interested in creative compositions, literary reviews and ELT.

Shouvik Narayan Hore has published two books of poetry, *The Horizon of Thoughts* and *Poet's Choice* (Book Two). He has been previously published in *The Pinewood Review* (USA), *Taj Mahal Review* and *Harvests of New Millennium* (IND). He is currently an editor of *The Literary Voyage*.

Carol J. Jennings is a lawyer and poet residing in Washington DC. Her first poetry collection, *The Dead Spirits at the Piano*, will be published by Cherry Grove Collections in 2016.

Abhay K. is a poet-diplomat. Winner of the SAARC Literary Award 2013 and nominated for the Pushcart Prize 2013, he is author of two memoirs and five collection of poems. He is currently editing *CAPITALS* - a poetry anthology on capital cities of the world. His work can be found at www.abhayk.com

Jasmine Kang is an artist/ writer who lives in California. Her poems on Kashmir pay respect to Kashmir and the struggle that the people of Kashmir are going through. Someday she hopes to visit Kashmir and experience its beauty. For more about Jasmine and her creative work please visit: http://moonshinegarden.com

John Lambremont Sr. is a poet from Baton Rouge, Louisiana, U.S.A. His poems have been published worldwide in many reviews and anthologies, including *Clarion* and *Picayune*.

Sonnet Mondal is an Indian Poet and editor. He was featured in the Famous Five in *India Today* magazine in 2010 and was long listed in "The Forbes Magazine's top 100 Celebrities 2014 edition" among India's most celebrated authors. He is the Founder of *The Enchanting Verses Literary Review* and is on the editorial board of the multilingual magazine *Levure littéraire* based in Paris, France.

Roseville Nidea is a poet from the Philippines. Her poetry has appeared in anthologies published in Canada and USA. Writing to preserve the tradition. She says, "To be part of Journeys Along the Silk Road is not merely my validation of being a fine poet, it is also an honour and a privilege to be heard. Mine is only a small voice singing for the love of my culture, of my tradition which is already on the brink of extinction because of the changes brought about by globalisation."

Kushal Poddar is presently living at Kolkata and writing poetry, fictions and others when not engaged in his day job as a lawyer in Calcutta. He authored, *The Circus Came To My Island* and his forthcoming books are *Kafka Dreamed Of Paprika* and *A Place For Your Ghost Animals.*

P.J.Reed is a writer and poet from England. She writes mainly in the dark romantic, supernatural and horror genres. Her work is found in many anthologies and writing guides. She has published one collection of poetry entitled *The Wicked Come.* For more information please visit her Facebook page at
https://www.facebook.com/pages/PJReed-Dark-Romantic-Poet

Elisavietta Ritchie has lived in Malaysia and Australia. She has visited to Indonesia, Singapore, Philippines, Thailand Japan, South Korea, to give readings and meet with their poets. She has published 16 Books. Her Latest is the *Tiger Upstairs On Connecticut Avenue*. For further information please visit her site at:
www.elisaviettaritchie.com

Kristin Roahrig's short stories and poetry have appeared in various publications. She is also the author of several plays and lives in Indiana.

Aditya Shankar is an Indian English poet living in

Bangalore and his work has been published in *Shot Glass Journal, Asiawrites, Indian Literature, Chandrabhaga, Munyori, The Pyramid, Poetry Chain, Meadowland Review, CHEST,* and *Vox Humana* among others. His latest poetry collection is *Party Poopers.*

Mumbai-based, **Sunil Sharma,** a college principal, is also a widely-published Indian critic, poet, literary interviewer, editor, translator, essayist and fiction writer. He has published three collections of poetry, one collection of short fiction, one novel and co-edited five books. His six short stories and the novel *Minotaur* were recently prescribed for the undergraduate classes of Post-colonial Studies, Clayton University, Georgia, USA. He is the recipient of the UK-based Destiny Poets' inaugural Poet of the Year award of 2012. He edits the online journal Episteme: http://www.episteme.net.in

Luna-Kleya Swart is an aspiring writer, avid reader, cat owner, mail artist, Zen enthusiast and daughter to a most wonderful mother.

Con Valenzuela is an English educator by profession. She is the Administrative Head of the Online English School in the Philippines. She writes grammar books for Korean students and edits eBook articles. She is also a published poet. She draws her poetic inspiration from her favourite poet Emily Dickinson.

Patricia Williams, a retired Professor of Design at the University of Wisconsin, has been published in on-line and print journals in both the US and UK including *Camel Saloon, Lake City Lights, Fox Cry, Middlebrow, Poetry*

Quarterly, *Red Booth Review*, *Third Wednesday* and others. Her work has been nominated for Best-of-the-Net and has been chosen for several other "Best of" publications.

Martin Willitts Jr. is a retired Librarian. He has poems in other Lost Tower Publications, as well as other poetry magazines. He has written 28 chapbooks and 10 full length collections of poetry.

Cigeng Zhang is a freelance English translator from Beijing. She started writing English poems online two years ago. Her Poem 'A Civet Cat' was published in *Purrfect Poetry* in 2014.

Photograph Credits

The great wall in the mist China	by Pixattitude from Dreamstime	12
Stone Guardian at Sewu Temple, Indonesia	An image of a stone guardian at the ancient Indonesian heritage temple of Sewu, located at Yogyakarta, Indonesia. The photograph was taken by Shariff Che'' Lah from Kuala Lumpur, Malaysia and bought from Dreamstime	33
Hamarikyu Garden, Japan	Kelly Kobayashi is an award-winning author of speculative/fantasy fiction. Her short story 'The Christmas Table' was recently published in the time-travel anthology *Of Past and Future*, and she is now working on a new steampunk series Although storytelling is her first love, travel and photography help to provide inspiration.	37
Petronas Twin Towers, Malaysia	The Petronas Twin Towers are an internationally recognised landmark in Kuala Lumpur, Malaysia and were the tallest buildings in the world from 1998 to 2004. This photograph was taken by Supannee Hickman of Huntington Park, United States	43
The Giant Buddha *Vietnam*	Giant Buddha, Gal Vihara, Polonnaruwa, Sri Lanka	53

street market lady seller	The photograph of the street market lady was taken in Hanoi, Vietnam by Aoshivn and bought from Dreamstime.	62

Made in the USA
Middletown, DE
01 October 2017